PARALLEL LANGUAGE LEARNING

APPRENDIMENTO PARALLELO DELLE LINGUE

Colourful Foods

Cibi Variopinti

ENGLISH/ITALIAN Vol.2

INGLESE/ITALIANO Vol.2

Lori Michelini

**Parallel Language Learning
Colourful Foods
English / Italian Volume 2**

**Apprendimento Parallelo delle Lingue
Cibi Variopinti
Inglese / Italiano Volume 2**

by Lori Michelini

PARALLEL LANGUAGE LEARNING

APPRENDIMENTO PARALLELO DELLE LINGUE

Colourful Foods

Cibi Variopinti

ENGLISH/ITALIAN Vol.2

INGLESE/ITALIANO Vol.2

Lori Michelini

Hi!
My name is
Lucy.
Today we're
going to show
you some
colourful foods.

Ciao!
Mi chiamo
Luca.
Oggi vi
mostreremo
alcuni
cibi variopinti.

However, is the word in English written as **COLOUR** or **COLOR?**

Allora, la parola in inglese si scrive **COLOUR** o **COLOR?**

People in Britain usually write it like this: **COLOUR**

La gente in Gran Bretagna di solito la scrive così: **COLOUR**

People in the United States instead write it like this: **COLOR**

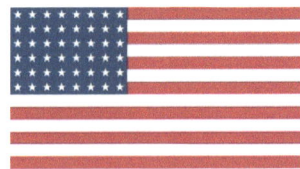

La gente negli Stati Uniti invece la scrive così: **COLOR**

But we're
hungry!
Shall we get
started?

Let's go!

Ma noi
abbiamo fame!
Possiamo
cominciare?

Andiamo!

In Italian, the colour usually comes after the food.

Yellow Bananas ⟷ Banane Gialle

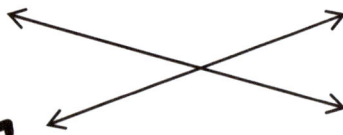

In inglese, il colore di solito viene dopo il cibo.

Yellow Banana ⟷ Banana Gialla

How do you say that?

Come si dice questo?

Gialle - *jahl-leh*

Yellow - *ielo*

Gialla - *jahl-lah*

Bananas - *bananas* ⟷ Banane - *bah-nah-neh*

Banana - *banana* ⟷ Banana - *bah-nah-nah*

I eat a banana at **BREAKFAST** (brecfast)

Io mangio una banana a **COLAZIONE** (koh-lah-zyo-nay)

Orange
Carrots

Carote
Arancioni

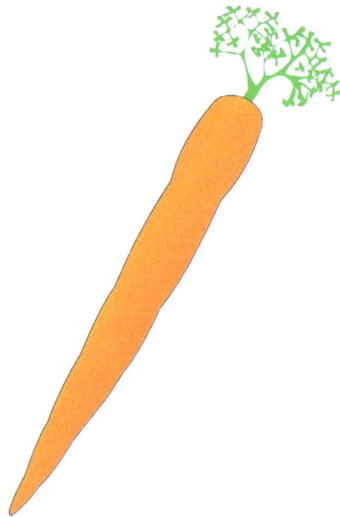

Orange
Carrot

Carota
Arancione

How do you say that?

Come si dice questo?

Orange - *oreng* ← Arancioni – *ah-rahn-choh-nee*

Arancione – *ah-rahn-choh-neh*

Carrots - *cherots* ←→ Carote – *kah-roh-teh*

Carrot - *cherot* ←→ Carota – *kah-roh-tah*

I eat carrots at **LUNCH** (lanc)

Io mangio carote a **PRANZO** (prahn-zoh)

Brown → Cioccolatini
Chocolates → Marroni

Brown → Cioccolato
Chocolate → Marrone

How do you say that?

Come si dice questo?

Brown - *braun*

Marroni – *mahr-roh-nee*

Marrone – *mahr-roh-neh*

Chocolates - *ciocolats* ⟷ Cioccolatini – *choke-koh-lah-tee-nee*

Chocolate - *ciocolat* ⟷ Cioccolato – *choke-koh-lah-toe*

I eat chocolate after **DINNER** (diner)

Io mangio cioccolato dopo **CENA** (chay-nah)

Purple → Uva

Grapes → Viola

Purple → Acino

Grape → Viola

How do you say that?

Come si dice questo?

Purple - *pörpol* ←——————→ Viola – *veeoh-lah*

Grapes - *greips* ←——————→ Uva – *ooh-vah*

Grape - *greip* ←——————→ Acino – *àh-chee-no*

Sometimes I eat grapes for **DESSERT** (dessert)

A volte io mangio uva per **DOLCE** (dohl-cheh)

Red
Tomatoes

Pomodori
Rossi

Red
Tomato

Pomodoro
Rosso

How do you say that?

Come si dice questo?

Rossi – *rohs-see*

Red - *red*

Rosso – *rohs-so*

Tomatoes - *tometos* ←——→ Pomodori – *poh-moh-doh-ree*

Tomato - *tometo* ←——→ Pomodoro – *poh-moh-doh-roh*

I like tomatoes in my **SALAD** (salad)

A me piacciono i pomodori nella mia **INSALATA** (een-sah-lah-tah)

Green Cucumbers → Cetrioli Verdi

Green Cucumber → Cetriolo Verde

How do you say that?

Come si dice questo?

Green - *grin*

Verdi – *vehr-dee*

Verde – *vehr-deh*

Cucumbers - *chiucambers* ←→ Cetrioli – *che-tree-oh-lee*

Cucumber - *chiucamber* ←→ Cetriolo – *che-tree-oh-low*

Cucumbers are healthy **to eat** (*tu it*)

I cetrioli sono salutari da **mangiare** (*mun-jah-reh*)

Black
Olives

Olive
Nere

Black
Olive

Oliva
Nera

How do you say that?

Come si dice questo?

Black - *bläc* → Nere – *neh-reh*

Black - *bläc* → Nera – *neh-rah*

Olives - *olivs* ←→ Olive – *oh-lee-veh*

Olive - *oliv* ←→ Oliva – *oh-lee-vah*

In Italy, olives are often eaten as a meal **STARTER** (starter)

In Italia, le olive vengono spesso mangiate come **ANTIPASTO** (ahn-tee-pah-sto)

White Eggs → Uova Bianche

White Egg → Uovo Bianco

How do you say that?

Come si dice questo?

White - *uait* ← Bianche – *be-ahn-keh*

Bianco – *be-ahn-koh*

Eggs - *egs*

Egg - *eg* ← Uovo – *woh-voh*

If the egg is **brown**, how would you say it in Italian?

Se l'uovo è **marrone**, come lo diresti in inglese?

Grey/Gray Fish → Pesci Grigi

Grey/Gray Fish → Pesce Grigio

How do you say that?

Come si dice questo?

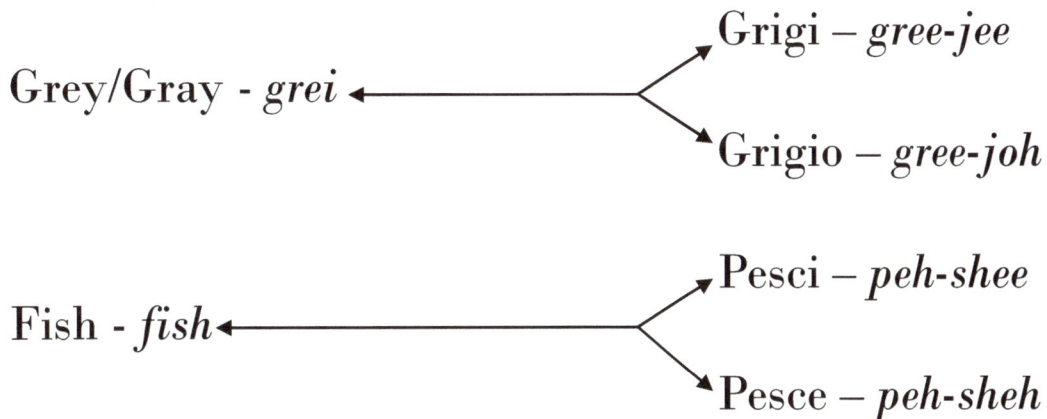

Grey/Gray - *grei*

→ Grigi – *gree-jee*

↘ Grigio – *gree-joh*

Fish - *fish*

↗ Pesci – *peh-shee*

↘ Pesce – *peh-sheh*

Fish is usually served on a **PLATE** (*pleit*)

Il pesce viene solitamente servito su un **PIATTO** (*pee-aht-toe*)

Pink   Torte

Cakes   Rosa

Pink   Torta

Cake   Rosa

How do you say that?

Come si dice questo?

Pink - *pinc* ←——————→ Rosa – *roh-zah*

Cakes - *cheics* ←——————→ Torte – *tor-teh*

Cake - *cheic* ←——————→ Torta – *tor-tah*

I eat cake with a **FORK** (forc)

Io mangio la torta con la **FORCHETTA** (for-ket-tah)

Blue
Ice Creams

Gelati
Azzurri

Blue
Ice Cream

Gelato
Azzurro

How do you say that?

Come si dice questo?

Blue - *blu* ←

Azzurri – *ahz-zoor-ree*

Azzurro – *ahz-zoor-roh*

Ice Creams – *ais crims* ←→ Gelati – *jeh-lah-tee*

Ice Cream – *ais crim* ←→ Gelato – *jeh-lah-toe*

In Italy, ice cream is often an afternoon **SNACK**. (*snäc*)

In Italia, il gelato è spesso una **MERENDA** (*meh-ren-dah*)

In Italian **Azzurro** isn't the only word for **"Blue."** There is also:

Celeste
and
Blu

What's the difference?

In inglese c'è solo una parola per il colore **"Blue."** Potrebbe essere descritto come:

Sky Blue
e
Deep Blue

Qual'è la differenza?

Sky Blue
(scai blu)

Celeste
(che-leh-steh)

Blue
(blu)

Azzurro
(ahz-zoor-roh)

Deep Blue
(dip blu)

Blu
(bloo)

Now, let's show
you some other
foods, but we
will not tell you
the colour.

Ora vi
mostriamo altri
cibi, ma non vi
diremo
il colore.

Can you see if you can remember the colours in Italian?

Vuoi vedere se riesci a ricordare come si dice il colore in inglese?

Crisps *or*
Potato Chips ←————————————→ Patatine

Crisp *or*
Potato Chip ←————————————→ Patatina

How do you say that?

Come si dice questo?

Crisps - *crisps*
Potato Chips – *poteto cips* ⟷ Patatine - *pah-tah-tee-neh*

Crisp - *crisp*
Potato Chip – *poteto cip* ⟷ Patatina – *pah-tah-tee-nah*

I like to eat my potato chips from a **BOWL** (bol)

Mi piace mangiare le mie patatine da una **CIOTOLA** (cho-toe-lah)

Meat  Carni

Meat  Carne

How do you say that?

Come si dice questo?

Meat - *mit* ⟷ Carni – *kahr-nee*

Meat - *mit* ⟷ Carne – *kahr-neh*

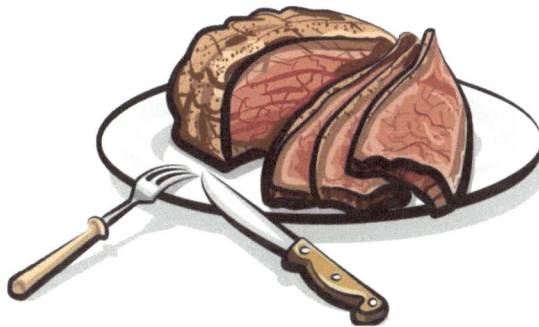

I eat meat with a **KNIFE** *(naif)* and a fork.

Io mangio la carne con **COLTELLO** *(kohl-tel-loh)* e forchetta

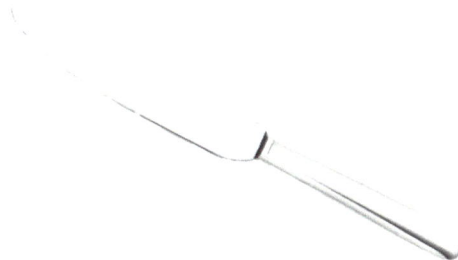

Soups  Zuppe

Soup  Zuppa

How do you say that?

Come si dice questo?

Soups - *sups* ⟷ Zuppe – *zoop-peh*

Soup - sup ⟷ Zuppa– *zoop-pah*

I eat soup with a **SPOON** (*spun*)

Io mangio la zuppa con il **CUCCHIAIO** (*kook-keeyah-yoh*)

Puddings $\longleftrightarrow$ Budini

Pudding $\longleftrightarrow$ Budino

How do you say that?

Come si dice questo?

Puddings - *pudins* ⟷ Budini – *boo-dee-nee*

Pudding - *pudin* ⟷ Budino – *boo-dee-no*

I eat pudding with a **TEASPOON** (*tespun*)

Io mangio il buddino con il **CUCCHIAINO** (*kook-keeyah-ee-no*)

Rice ←——————→ Riso

Grain of Rice ←——→ Chicco di Riso

How do you say that?

Come si dice questo?

Rice - *rais* ←————————→ Riso – *ree-zoh*

Grain of Rice – *grein of rais* ←——→ Chicco – *keek-koh*

I eat rice with **CHOPSTICKS** (ciopstics)

Io mangio il riso con le **BACCHETTE** (bahk-ket-teh)

Hamburgers ⟵ Hamburger

In Italian, you say just "Hamburger" whether it's one hamburger or two... or three.

Hamburger ⟷ Hamburger

How do you say that?

Come si dice questo?

Hamburgers - *hämbürghers* ⟷ Hamburger – *hambùrger*

Hamburger - *hämbürgher* ⟷ Hamburger – *hambùrger*

> I eat hamburgers with my **HANDS** (*händs*)

> Io mangio gli hamburger con le **MANI** (*mah-nee*)

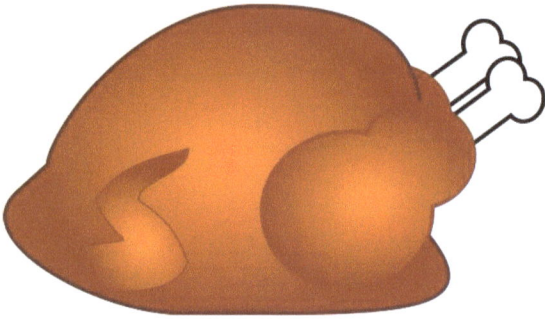 

Roast
Chickens

Polli
Arrosto

Fried
Chicken

Pollo
Fritto

How do you say that?

Come si dice questo?

Chickens - *cicchens*

Chicken - *cicchen*

Polli- *pohl-lee*

Pollo – *pohl-loh*

Do you like **ROAST** chicken (rost) or **FRIED** chicken? (fraid)

Ti piace il pollo **ARROSTO** (ahr-roh-sto) o il pollo **FRITTO**? (freet-toe)

Lettuces ⟵⟶ Lattughe

Lettuce ⟵⟶ Lattuga

How do you say that?

Come si dice questo?

Lettuces - *letases*

Lettuce - *letas*

Lattughe – *laht-too-geh*

Lattuga – *laht-too-gah*

Lettuce is a **VEGETABLE** (*végetebol*) you can grow in your garden.

La lattuga è una **VERDURA** (*vehr-doo-rah*) che puoi coltivare nel tuo orto.

Sandwiches $\longleftrightarrow$ Panini

Sandwich $\longleftrightarrow$ Panino

How do you say that?

Come si dice questo?

Sandwiches - *sänduices* ⟷ Panini – *pah-nee-nee*

Sandwich - *sänduic* ⟷ Panino – *pah-nee-no*

I like **CHEESE** (cis) Sandwiches

Mi piacciono i panini al **FORMAGGIO** (for-maj-joe)

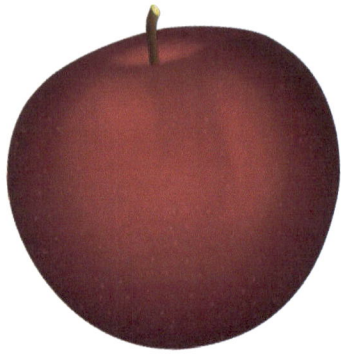 

Apples  Mele

Apple  Mela

How do you say that?

Come si dice questo?

Apples - *äpols* ⟷ Mele – *meh-leh*

Apple - *äpol* ⟷ Mela – *meh-lah*

Apples are a type of **FRUIT** *(frut)* that grows on trees.

Le mele sono un tipo di **FRUTTA** *(froot-tah)* che cresce sugli alberi.

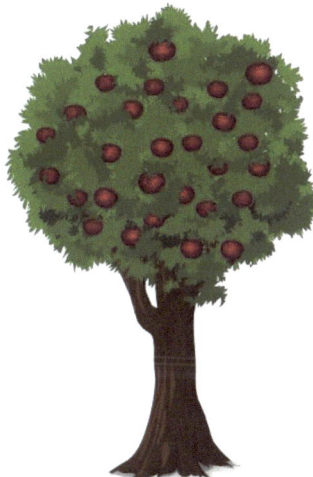

Oranges ←——————————→ Arance

Orange ←——————————→ Arancia

How do you say that?

Come si dice questo?

Oranges - *orenges* ⟷ Arance – *ah-run-chay*

Orange - *oreng* ⟷ Arancia – *ah-run-cha*

Oranges make good **orange juice** (*oreng gius*)

Le arance fanno un buon **succo d'arancia** (*sook-koh dah-run-cha*)

There are so
many more
foods we could
tell you about.
But we're not
hungry
anymore.
So, until next
time...
Arrivederci!

Ci sono così
tanti altri cibi
di cui potremmo
parlarti.
Ma non abbiamo
più fame.
Quindi, fino
alla prossima
volta...
Goodbye!

Please leave a short review of this book on Amazon!

Per favore lascia una breve recensione su Amazon!

Also in this series...

Inoltre in questa serie...

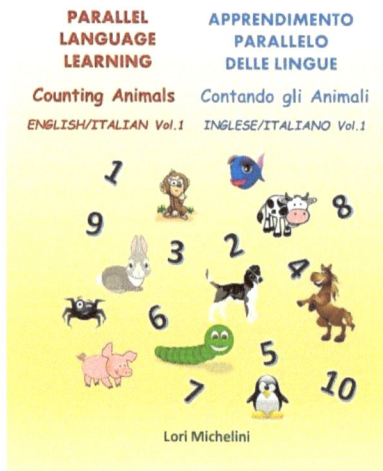

PARALLEL LANGUAGE LEARNING

APPRENDIMENTO PARALLELO DELLE LINGUE

Counting Animals — Contando gli Animali

ENGLISH/ITALIAN Vol.1 — INGLESE/ITALIANO Vol.1

Lori Michelini

PARALLEL LANGUAGE LEARNING

APPRENDIMENTO PARALLELO DELLE LINGUE

Things at Home — Cose a Casa

ENGLISH/ITALIAN Vol.3 — INGLESE/ITALIANO Vol.3

Lori Michelini

PARALLEL LANGUAGE LEARNING

APPRENDIMENTO PARALLELO DELLE LINGUE

City and Country — Città e Campagna

ENGLISH/ITALIAN Vol.4 — INGLESE/ITALIANO Vol.4

Lori Michelini

PARALLEL LANGUAGE LEARNING

APPRENDIMENTO PARALLELO DELLE LINGUE

Jobs and Professions — Mestieri e Professioni

ENGLISH/ITALIAN Vol.5 — INGLESE/ITALIANO Vol.5

Lori Michelini

www.lorimichelini.com

Also / Anche

Facebook &
Instagram

www.ingramcontent.com/pod-product-compliance
Lightning Source LLC
LaVergne TN
LVHW072052070426
835508LV00002B/59